Families

Families

A Celebration of Diversity, Commitment, and Love

Aylette Jenness

Photographs by the author

Houghton Mifflin Company
Boston 1990

Library of Congress Cataloging-in-Publication Data

Jenness, Aylette.
  Families : a celebration of diversity, commitment, and love /
Aylette Jenness.
    p.   cm.
  Bibliography: p.
  Summary: Photographs and text depict the lives of seventeen
families from around the country, some with step relationships,
divorce, gay parents, foster siblings, and other diverse
components. The material was originally a traveling exhibition,
begun at the Children's Museum in Boston.
  ISBN 0-395-47038-2
  1. Family—United States—Exhibitions—Juvenile
literature.   2. Photography of families—Exhibitions—Juvenile
literature.   3. Children's Museum of Boston—Exhibitions—
Juvenile literature.
[1. Family life.]   I. Title.   89-7507
HQ536.J46   1989   CIP
306.85′074′73—dc20   AC

Printed in the United States of America

H   10 9 8 7 6 5 4 3 2 1

To Elaine Heumann Gurian, who started this,
and to Sam Bowles, who sustained it,

and to that battered, joyous, struggling, evolving,
and sustaining institution — the family

Acknowledgments

Many thanks are due to:

The fine families who are pictured here, and to the kids in particular, who so generously overcame shyness and privacy to share their lives with us all.

Elaine Heumann Gurian, past director of the Exhibit Center of The Children's Museum, Boston, whose support, ideas, and belief in this project made it all possible.

The staff at The Children's Museum, who discussed the issues, sent me to possible participants, and designed and produced the exhibit from which this book came.

The principal and teachers at the Runkle Elementary School in Brookline, Massachusetts, for incorporating the exhibit into their curriculum, and sharing the results with me.

The students at the Black Pine Circle School in Berkeley, California, who told me their ideas about families.

My agent, Frances Goldin, my editor, Matilda Welter, and designer Susan Sherman.

My own family, for what I have learned from them: my parents, my brother and niece, my ex-husband and his family, my ex-and-thankfully-forever mother-in-law, my children and stepchildren and their spouses, my partner and his family, and, not least, my dearest friends.

Contents

Introduction

Families — what are they? Your family is the people who take care of you, who care about you. Your family may be the person who adopted you. Your family may be your birth mother or father. Your family may include people who joined you, like stepparents and stepbrothers and stepsisters. Your family may be your grandparents, your aunt or uncle, or your guardian. Some kids are able to ask friends to act as family for them — sometimes temporarily — and this can be a big help.

Families change over time. This can be painful, if you miss someone who's moved out of your life. In other ways, it's fine. At different times in your life, when you will have new needs and interests, you may find new people to call on.

Families are spread out over space. Members may move all over the world. You may be able to write to, or telephone, or visit, relatives who live in different kinds of places. It can be a big network you have, a way of learning about places far from your hometown.

Some people think a family is supposed to be a mom and a dad and their children. This can cause a lot of hurt feelings. In school, you may be asked to make a Mother's Day card; but lots of kids don't live with their mothers. You may be asked to bring your dad to work on the school playground for a day; but lots of kids don't live with their dads. Most kids know that, really, families are often very different from "Mom 'n' Dad".

And that "very different" can be a fine thing. A family of two can be close and cozy. A big family can mean there are many people to go to for help or for fun. A family that changes over time means there are different people to be with over your life. A family whose members are very different from each other means you can learn a wide variety of things.

What do *you* think a family is?

Here are some kids' answers to the question.

What makes a family is being loved. And cared for. And it do not matter how many people are in a family it could be from 2 - 10 +

Mariage, children, and many more things make families.

My dog and cat are really part of my family

Love can form a family. You don't even have to be related to the other person. You can have a baby or adopt a kid.

8

What do families do?

Families care for each other.
And they encourage each other.

Most families have quarrels

Family members help each other.

They get you into trouble.
They realy like eachother.

They provide for each other.
They watch out for one another.
They precaution for each other.
They only punish each other as much as they deserve - Never more, never less. No family is completely perfect - No fights, No arguements - etc. etc. etc.

What do you think the purpose of a family is, anyway?

The purpose of families is to teach people.

To have fun with each other.
If you have a brother or sister look after them.

Families are for company.

Families are for looking up to somebody.

The purpose of a family is to bring more people into the world. And to have someone to talk to.

On the following pages, seventeen kids will tell you about their families. How have they answered these questions? And how are they like your family? Different from your family?

9

Tam

Tam says, "I have a big family. Ari and Chessie aren't adopted, but the rest of us are. We were adopted when we were babies. Kri — she's up on the swing next to me — likes drawing rainbows. Ari — she's standing next to me in front of Mom — she likes to swim. Tasha's sitting on the ground in front of Ari. She likes horses. Chessie is two — she's in the little swing in front of Dad — she likes to name animals. I like dissecting things and trying out experiments.

"When someone in our family has a birthday, they get to pick out a dinner that they want, and they open presents at the end of the meal. Sometimes we buy the presents, and sometimes we make them. Everyone gets a lot of presents!"

Tam's mother says that from time to time, Tasha, Kri, and Tam have asked the questions that adopted children often ask: "Where did I come from? Who was my mother?" She explains that they were born to another woman, and as they've grown older, she talks about their ethnic backgrounds. But she emphasizes that *she* is their mother, their parent.

"A parent is a person who takes care of you, raises you, looks after you, and loves you," she says.

And that's what she and her husband are for Tasha, Kri, and Tam, just as they are for Ari and Chessie.

Hakem

"I live with my brother, Amos, and my mom. My grandfather and my grandmother and some of my aunts and cousins are my family, too, even though they live in a different place. I think I like it this way, because if my father was here, they might be fighting and stuff. My mom lets me do more than other moms do. And I do a lot of things with her.

"I play with Amos a lot. Sometimes I'm a little mean to him, 'cause he does stuff that other kids don't do — stuff that makes me mad. But when he's in a fight with one of his friends, I try to stop it."

Hakem's mother, Tamara, says that Hakem is very helpful with Amos — almost like a second mother. At the same time, she has many friends of her own. She plays the steel drums and she likes to paint. She does well in school, too.

Tamara says, "We are really very close. The kids were born at home, and I think this has made a connection which we still have.

"Life is sometimes hard for a single parent. If the goal is to help children grow the very best they can, then the single parent has even more responsibility to provide outside resources. I think music, art, and a consciousness of the natural world surrounding children helps them discover who they are and encourages a sense of responsibility to the earth and to other people. My children are wonderful, and I love them."

David

This is David's family in California — his brother, Mark, his mother, Bea, his mother's friend Larry, and his grandmother. He says, "My parents are divorced and my dad lives in New York. He's remarried, so I have a stepsister and a little half-brother and a little half-sister.

"My mother and my father are very different, and yet I'm so close to both of them that it doesn't matter anymore that they're divorced, except that I'd like to see my father more often."

David's mother is studying to be a college English teacher for deaf people. She herself is deaf. David says, "Some people ask me, do I accept my mother as a deaf mother? I always think that's kind of a strange question. I don't accept her as a deaf mother, I accept her just as my mother, deaf or not deaf, or black hair or brown hair, or anything. I consider her my mother, and then she has this special quality — she's deaf — and so sometimes there's things that I have to deal with, like taking phone calls for her.

"Sometimes I get really frustrated because I have to make phone calls for her if she wants to call someone who's hearing, and they don't have TTY. TTY is a machine attached to the telephone so people can type conversations to each other, and read them on a screen. If they don't have TTY, I have to talk for them, and it could be a person with an accent I have trouble understanding. Or for some reason I don't want to talk to that person.

But I have to do it and I accept that I have to do it, because she wouldn't ask it of me if she could do it herself. Often she tries to do it herself, if there's any way she can. It's not like she tries to depend on me, like I've heard some mothers do; she doesn't try to depend on me.

"There are things I have to do for her, and things she has to do for me, and we have to try a little harder because she's deaf, but it all works out.

"I learned sign language before I learned to speak, so there's no problem of communication. Just like babies learn English, I learned sign language, 'cause that's what my mother used; it was just a language that was used around the house. I picked it up. She didn't send me to a sign language course when I was a baby!

I'm learning Hebrew now, and I'm having trouble because any language you try to learn you'll have trouble with, but when you're a baby, you just pick it up.

"Very, very seldom have I been teased because my mother is deaf. Half of the kids in my class can do some finger spelling, and they want to do that. It's kind of nice to know finger spelling, it's just like if my mother knew another language. I've never felt embarrassed by that."

David's mother agrees. She signs, "I think my two boys are very proud of having a deaf mother. They're proud they can speak two languages, and they see two different cultures. It helps them be more sensitive. Not only to deaf culture and hearing culture, but they're also involved in gay culture, and different racial cultures, because we know a lot of different people. I grew up that way myself. I asked them a couple of days ago, 'If I wasn't deaf, would you still be proud of me?' And David said, 'Yeah, but I prefer that you're a deaf mother.' "

David has two special interests right now. He explains, "I draw. I want to be a cartoonist when I grow up. I think I'd like to do a daily comic strip or a greeting card thing or a commercial advertisement. If I couldn't do that, I'd wish I'd become a preschool teacher — I like little kids. I baby-sit. I love playing with my brother and my little brother and sisters in New York.

"I like cactuses 'cause there are so many different kinds of them. I take care of my little cactus garden. I even name them. There's Bulbs, because it's got bulbs, and Dick and Lois and there's Grizzly, and Goliath. It's kind of silly, but I like it. Other people name their plants, I think."

Laney

Laney belongs to a big Cuban-American family. Sixty-two relatives get together for special occasions! Here she's with the group who see each other regularly. They've gathered for the christening of Laney's newborn nephew — he's just a few weeks old. She's proud to be sitting between her mother and her aunt, and holding the baby on her lap.

"It's fun to be part of a big family," Laney says. "We go to a lot of parties, we go to a lot of christenings, we go to a lot of weddings. Some of us go to funerals — I don't, though — I don't like to. We go to graduations and graduation parties. We go to church together, and sometimes we get together after church. We go to confirmations if someone in the family is making a confirmation. We go to visit my great-grandmother, Abuela Amparo.

"I do different things with different people in my family. I go to the State House with my Uncle Roy — that's where he works — and to basketball games and to Latino festivals. He takes me to the amusement park, for the rides, and he takes me to get my hair cut.

"With my Aunt Susie, I mostly hang out at her house. Sometimes we go shopping, sometimes we go to the movies, sometimes we go to the park. I help her take care of the baby, but he's too young for me to take care of by myself. I'm kind of afraid I might drop him, 'cause I'm shaky, knowing he's a newborn, unless someone's standing right there when I'm holding him. When he's one or two I'll take care of him alone.

"With my grandmother, Mima, I watch television, and I go to work with her sometimes. Sometimes I stay over.

"I love my family very much because they're very nice to me. They make me happy when I'm sad, and when I'm sick they bring me presents, and they take good care of me."

Brian

"My sisters, Carina and Lianne, and me — I'm Brian, I'm the youngest — and my mother and my father; that's my family. I'm in the Cub Scouts. I like to play soccer in my free time. I play the guitar and the trumpet, too. I like astronomy; it seems sort of interesting to me. My dad's an engineer, he's involved in math a lot. My mom cooks and cleans the house, and in her free time, she reads. She's a secretary at my school when one of the other secretaries is out.

"I think my family cares about me more, because some other families let their kids go anywhere, and sometimes they don't care if they do their homework. Sometimes they don't care how messy their handwriting is. They let them go to their friends' houses, or invite their friends over. My family doesn't let me go out as often — but I don't mind that, I stay with my family more. I have to respect my sisters; I have to stay out of their room — it isn't a public room.

"In our free time, we go to a movie, or we go to Boston. Mostly we just stay around home. I like this house, I like the things that we do. I just really like everything that happens here."

Tina

Tina moved in with her adoptive family just a year ago. Here she is, sitting between her grandparents. Her mother, Helen, and her big brother are standing behind her.

Helen had always wanted to have a daughter — partly because she's always been close to her *own* mother. Helen's sons were grown, and she was divorced and teaching school when she decided to adopt a teenager. The social worker Helen had gone to showed the family a picture of Tina, and then they met. "I felt so excited," Helen says. Soon Tina moved into the house — as Helen says, "never to leave again — until *she* decides to."

The day Tina came was a big occasion. "She knew she was *it*," says Helen, "so we had a special party. It was a celebration of Tina."

"I even got presents," says Tina, "and I started my first bank account. It started with twenty-five dollars, and now it's up to a hundred and five. I put money in almost every month."

By now Tina is completely settled into her new family. "My mother cooks with me and takes me places. We go shopping together — mostly for food, but sometimes for junk. Gram does my hair and listens to me practice the piano. My brother takes me out for ice cream. And my grandfather sews my clothes when they need it."

Jaime

Jaime's father came to the United States from Mexico twelve years ago. At first he stayed with his uncle, and worked on a farm. There he began to learn English, and later he moved to California. Jaime's mother came from Mexico a little later, living with her brother until she met and married Jaime's father.

Now they have five sons — Jaime, Salvador, Javier, Gabriel, and Hector. Jaime and Salvador go to school, and Javier goes to a nursery school where both of his parents help the teacher each week. Gabriel and Hector are at home with their mother, where she is busy all the time, washing clothes, cooking, and cleaning for her big family.

Jaime's father has two jobs — he works full time in a restaurant, and part time as a janitor. He says, smiling, "Five kids — I've got to work a lot!"

A few months ago Jaime's whole family went back to Mexico for the first time to visit relatives. Jaime's father says, "I drove nearly fifty hours — two nights and three days." The boys got to know many family members they had never met, especially their grandparents.

Here in the United States, Jaime's family members speak Spanish to each other and to their Mexican-American friends. They speak English to people who can't understand Spanish. Jaime's father wants the boys to do well in school here. He says, "Some people like to get money, and that's it. I don't like that.

School is important. Maybe the boys will have a job like a mailman — or, why not, maybe a doctor or a lawyer."

Jaime likes his school, especially math class and using the computers. After school, he plays with his brothers. Sometimes he helps take care of his littlest brother, Hector. "I pick him up, give him toys, play games with him. Sometimes I help my mother — I clean my room. Sometimes I *don't* help my mother.

"I like playing with my friends — hand wrestling, tag, hide and seek, and soccer." Jaime is on a soccer team, and he practices twice a week after school.

What does he want to be when he grows up? He smiles at his father and says, "I want to be a lawyer."

Ananda

Ananda's family is her parents and the other members of her religious community, the Happy, Healthy, Holy Organization, with whom she lives.

"Early in the morning," Ananda says, "we all do *sadhana* together — that means exercises and meditation. Then we have *gurdwara* — that's a ceremony. First we sing songs, then we do *hukum* — that's reading a special book. After that we serve out *prasad* — that's a sweet pudding. And then I go to school."

The school bus picks her up near her ashram, a big quiet house in the country. She especially likes a gymnastics class she goes to. "Every week we do something different — we do the bars, the ropes, the trampolines, the rings."

After school, Ananda often brings a friend home with her. Her friends all like the glass animal collection she keeps safely up on a special shelf in her room. "In the winter I go sledding with my friends, and in the summer we pick blackberries and blueberries and come home and make a drink. We play with my cat, Narayan."

Ananda's father says of their home and family, "An ashram is a spiritual community where people practice a spiritual lifestyle with the goal of merging your will with God's will. This way you find peace and harmony within your life. We have regular jobs outside, but this is our home. It's a simple lifestyle, and very fulfilling."

Ananda says, "It's fine and fun. Otherwise I would be bored and not have anything to do."

Nhor

Nhor first met his foster father, David, in an airport, less than a year before this picture was taken. Nhor tells the story: "I was on the plane twenty-four hours from Thailand to California, from six o'clock in the morning until six o'clock the next day. When I saw David, I didn't know how to say, 'Nice to meet you' or anything like that. I only knew to say 'Hello.' "

David thought Nhor looked scared, and he *knew* that he himself was scared. He hadn't slept much the night before, knowing that Nhor was flying halfway around the world to his new home. Nhor's parents had died in Cambodia, and Nhor had lived for three years in a camp in Thailand until a new home was found for him in the United States.

Since then a lot has happened. Nhor has learned a new language and new customs. He goes to a big high school. "I have English, health, math, p.e., and study hall. I like all my courses. And I like sports — soccer, softball, roller skating. I like watching TV and going to the movies.

"I still have friends that I knew at the camp in Thailand. Now they're in Quebec, California, Virginia — all over. Sometimes I call them on the telephone."

At home, David and Nhor share the work. "I like washing dishes, cleaning the house, but I don't like to cook. I don't know how to cook, and I don't want to cook. I cut the grass." Luckily, David does like to cook. He has a book, *1001 Oriental Recipes*, from which he is learning to make some Cambodian dishes.

David feels strongly the responsibility he bears as a parent. "It's not to be taken lightly," he says. "It's very time consuming and involving. You have to realize you haven't shaped this person, that he has had other parents. But for me it's a fine experience. Nhor has made an incredible adjustment. Sometimes he's lonely since there are just the two of us. But on the other hand, I can give him a lot of attention."

Nhor says simply, "David is my family now."

Jeannette

"In my family," says Jeannette, "there's my mother, my father (he's away right now, that's why he isn't in the picture), my brothers, and Sonia and David. Sonia and David are my foster sister and brother.

"For about five years my mother's been taking in kids. They come to us because their parents can't take care of them, or they can but they don't know how, or they're having problems. They come and live with us for we don't know how long, and my mom, she takes care of them. The agency says, 'Try not to get attached,' but you can't help but get attached to them.

"Sonia's been with us for three and a half years. She came to us when she was a little baby. She wouldn't talk to anybody when she first came, but then she got out of her shell. Now she talks to everybody, 'cause she knows that they love her.

"David was with us for four and a half years. Then he was adopted by Jeri. He loves Jeri and he has a new grandmother and a new grandfather. It was hard to let him go — it hurt to see him leave — but my mother said he didn't really leave 'cause he's just up the hill over at Jeri's. And he still is, he is my brother.

"I baby-sit for my mother, and I watch the kids when I come home from school if my mother has to go out. I know how to take care of babies. The only thing I don't like is I hate changing their stinky diapers. I do like playing with them.

"But when I grow up, I'm going to be a cosmetologist, or an accountant, or work in a bank. I'm in the eighth grade now and I'm interested in going to Boston Latin School or Boston Technical High."

Elliott

Elliott's family is his two fathers — his "Papa," Dmitri, and his "Daddy," Tom. Dmitri says, "Families come in all shapes and sizes. We happen to be gay men, two men who love each other, but we do the same things that other families do — we make oatmeal for Elliott, we give him baths."

"Dmitri and I knew when we first got together nine years ago that we wanted to be parents," Tom explains. "We started to prepare for a family long before Elliott was born. That's why we bought our house."

"Elliott was adopted at birth," Dmitri says. "His birth mother wasn't able to raise him. Elliott knows her. He sees her from time to time, and he'll be able to ask her questions when he wants to. He'll always have a relationship with her.

"We were in the hospital when Elliott was born, and we brought him home, here, from the hospital. I think that our way of being open about our family helped people accept us. We'd be out pushing the baby carriage in our neighborhood, and neighbors would say, 'Oh, you've got a baby? Congratulations!' We try to make ourselves approachable, so people can ask us questions if they want to.

"We've split up taking care of Elliott pretty evenly," Dmitri continues. "If he gets hurt, he'll run to one of us, say me — I'll pick him up, and then he'll turn to Tom." Dmitri goes to work very early each morning, so Tom helps Elliott get dressed and takes him to his day-care center.

"I like my teachers," Elliott says. "I like it when we read stories in school, and I like drawing and tracing and coloring." Dmitri picks Elliott up and spends the afternoon with him.

"After school I play with my Lego farm," says Elliott. "I paint at my easel. I have a smock. And I like to play Sesame Street on the computer. I can put in the disk. Then I push ENTER. I can make numbers and animals on the computer. I can spell my name, E-L-L-I-O-T-T. You have to be careful. You never shake the computer!"

When Tom comes home, he cooks Elliott's dinner and puts him to bed. "And every night, we sing 'Goodnight, Sweetheart,' " Dmitri says. "Together.

"You know," Dmitri goes on, "I'd like to have six kids. I came from a family of four kids, and I love my siblings. I want Elliott to have that, too. The most I've gotten Tom to commit to is four; I may

have to come down a little. Maybe five."

Tom and Dmitri have begun to make it known that they're available to adopt another child who needs a family. "I want a baby brother!" says Elliott.

Right now they're looking for a bigger house with a bigger yard. Big enough for their three dogs. And — who knows — maybe five kids.

Dmitri says. "We're really not so different from other families. Sometimes adults have more preconceived notions than kids do. The other day I was picking up Elliott at school, and a little girl came up to me. She said, 'Are you Elliott's daddy?' I said, 'Yes.' She said, 'Then who's Tom?' I said, 'He's Elliott's daddy, too.' 'Oh,' she said. Then, almost to herself, 'Elliott's got two daddies. I haven't got any!' "

Eve

"**I** mostly live with my mom," Eve says, "but about two nights a week I go to my dad and my stepmom's house, and I live there and I go to school from there. I have my own room in each house, and in both houses I have desks where I can do my homework.

"I have two brothers, but they're both away at school. And I have a dog, Lion.

"In Dad's house, it's Dad's way, and in Mom's house, it's Mom's way. I've realized that they're different parents, and I shouldn't treat them the same. But sometimes it gets into problems for myself. If I like rules from one house better than the other, I feel like saying, 'I

like it better when you do it *this* way.' But I try to work it out. I usually say, 'Well, I know this is your rules, but I wonder if you would rewrite the rules a little, because I'm disagreeing with some of them.'

"My mom pushes me a lot in my homework, and it helps, 'cause she really makes me do it. At my dad's it's a little bit like, 'Okay, let's do this together.' At my mom's there's more expected of me, and at my dad's there's more done for me. Those are very different, but they're a nice contrast. I like them both.

"When my dad first got married, it was a little hard, because I thought I was expected to treat my stepmother like Mom, but then I realized I didn't have to. I love them both, but I know more about my mom; I know what's going to happen

more. With my stepmom, I have to think a little more, or ask a little more, because she's a lot newer in my life. My mom likes my stepmother, and how she treats me, and my stepmother respects my mom. I consider myself real lucky."

Jody

"I have more than one family," Jody says. "There's my father and his family, and I have a brother, too. Then there's my mom and Carole and me.

"I get along with my mom really well, and I love her a lot. But when she first decided she was going to be a lesbian, I was hysterical. I was totally freaked out. I was just like, 'Can't you wait till I leave home? It's fine for your life, and I want you to do what you need, but not while I'm still here.' I didn't want any of my friends to know, and it's still scary for me telling even a close friend — I'm scared they won't want to come to my house, or they'll go, 'Oh, gross,' or not say it, but think it.

"When I first met Carole I hated her a lot, even though I didn't know her. But Carole is a really neat person, and the more I got to know her, the more thrilled I was to be around her. Somehow it was easier for me to see her as part of my family because I wasn't expected to, I didn't feel pressure. I could claim her as a parent, that was between the two of us.

"Now I love having Carole here. I love being with her. I don't think about what's lesbian and what's straight, it's just Carole and my mom. I can see how happy my mom is, how happy Carole is, how they're just two people loving each other.

"I can call on Carole any time for any reason, it could be serious or not serious. If I'm upset about things, I can call on her, it could be any time of day or night.

If I need somebody to take me somewhere or do something with me, she'll help me. And we like to go shopping and to the movies together. We have an independent relationship. I feel like she's a real parent to me. And if anything happened to me, she would take care of me.

"I told one of my very close friends a while ago. I said it real casually: 'Oh, did you know my mom's a lesbian?' And it turns out — I don't know if she changed her mind, or if that was what she'd been thinking all along — but she's started standing up for gay people, and speaking out for gay rights. You know, there's no one characteristic that would define lesbians, it's just different people. I'm

34

looking at these people — they could be glamorous Miss Americas or senior queens — anybody could be a lesbian.

Anyway, I thought that was really nice. My friend gets in a lot of arguments for being pro-gay."

Adam

"The head of the family is the big momma," Adam says with a smile. "Then there's my brother, Eric, who's twenty-two and doesn't live with us now, then my sisters, Jessie and Emily, and me. And Zoe, our cat.

"When I was ten, my dad died. That's the worst thing that can happen, of course, and for a while I was afraid of a lot of things happening. But now we've adjusted to it, and we're all right. In fact, I'd say we're a very happy family.

"There's a lot of center around Mom, which can be bad, because it means that she's getting involved in every dispute, which isn't fair to her. But we're all capable of working out our own problems separate from her. We're dependent on each other, but at the same time, we can deal with things alone.

"I think the strength of our family is that usually nothing is hidden. If someone is upset, it's known and worked out. We're far from a perfect family, and there's conflicts, and there can be a lot of emotion. But that should be expected, because it's a learning process to go through that, and I think it's really important. There's always a lot of affection and support involved in this family.

"For me, having a home like this is really something I want to come back to every day. It's a comfort and security, and there's a nice lightness. You can loosen up and be completely yourself."

Mattie

Mattie lives with her parents, Alice and Billy, her son, Isaiah, and her sister and brothers in a Yup'ik Eskimo town in Alaska.

"When my mom and dad first heard I was pregnant," Mattie says, "they weren't happy about it. They used to talk. Seemed like they didn't care if they put me down. They made it look like they didn't care — but they really did.

"Now I stay home most of the time with my baby," she goes on. "I help my mom with the housework. Same old thing every day, it never changes. Sometimes when I want to go out, my mom says no one will watch Isaiah, and I get mad, I want to go out. Just get mad for no reason. Sometimes I feel like moving out, being on my own. But then when I try, it's hard. I want to come back.

"Sometimes when problems come, a lot of problems pile in my head and I feel like committing suicide. But then I think of my parents; I'd hurt them, and they'd blame themselves for what I did. Killing yourself for problems, it wouldn't solve anything. I have other friends who thought of suicide. It's better if we just talk to our parents about our problems, instead of ignoring it. When I do that, I feel better inside of me."

And meanwhile, her parents are planning to raise Isaiah. Theirs is a strong, lively, and loving family, warmly looking after the new baby. To Mattie's parents, Billy and Alice, nothing is more

important than their family. Their goal is to keep each child well clothed, fed, cared for, and taught to survive.

Alice says, "Billy always talked of adopting, he always wanted to raise more kids. But at first the other kids thought it wouldn't be good to have a baby at home. After, they were happy. Those young uncles, they like having a baby around. and it makes me feel good to have the kids loving a baby again."

When Mattie has free time, she loves to play basketball in the town gym. She's on the women's team, and she's a good

player. She's planning to go back to high school when Isaiah is a little older. She hopes to go on to college when she graduates. She'll be the first person in her family to attend college, and she's proud of her plans for the future.

Jody

"I think I was about four when my parents got divorced," says Jody. "My dad lived in Boston, and I'd go up and visit him on the weekend. Then he decided he'd move here so he could be with me more. I thought that was terrific. He got a nice house, and it's pretty near me. He used to work for the State House, and now he works here. I can bike over to his house, and he can come pick me up to do something. My dad's the coach of my soccer team, and he's the president of the league. We play soccer every Sunday. In this picture, he's standing behind me.

"In my family now, there's my stepfather, Ted, my mother, Didi, my half-sister, Sarah, my dad, Dave, our pony, Peaches, our cat Shadow, our cat Cindy, our cat Mystery, our cat Sodapop, and our dog, Flash. We got Flash a month or so ago. He's a golden retriever. He's pretty young, and he's really nice.

"We do a lot of family projects with my mom. With Ted, my stepdad, I like to make things. He used to be a mechanic, and he helps me fix up my bike, and stuff like that.

"I'm interested in aikido now. And I'm starting the drums — that's really great!"

41

Jennifer

Jennifer lives with her mother and her sister, Merryn, in a commune — a household of people who have chosen to share a home. Her family includes two other small families right now — and Tiger Lily, her cat. Here Jen and Merryn are sitting on the floor in their living room, with their mother behind Merryn.

"I've lived here in this house since I was three. It's always seemed right to me. I love it. I'd be lonelier if it was just my mom and Merryn and me. In this house you make more friends, you meet more people. Of course, it's hard when people leave — they're family, they really *are* family — and you get really close to them. There's a list of about fifty people who've lived here. They come back to visit.

"We have a hard time trying to find new people to move in, 'cause we have to get to know them, we have to see if they can fit into our family style. And everyone has to agree on someone. And of course, *they* have to like it, too."

Family members share housework, help each other in a variety of ways, and spend a lot of time together. "They help me with schoolwork — Jerry's good at math — and they give me rides. We go shopping together, or to the movies. And I'll do favors for them — I baby-sit for Sam, I help them out.

"I love my family. I can't imagine living anywhere else."

In Conclusion

Each of the kids in this book has learned some important things about families. Adam knows that you can survive the death of your parent. Jody (the girl) knows that you can grow to love someone you thought you'd hate. Ananda and Jennifer and Laney have all found that turning to one of a large number of people can be helpful. Hakem values the closeness and attention of a very small family. David knows that a "handicap" isn't always a handicap — it can be a source of strength and power. Brian sees that his parents' rules are protective. Eve has learned to live with, and benefit from, two very different sets of rules.

They all know that it isn't important who makes up the family; what's important is how members feel about each other, and what they do for each other.

At best, family members are committed to each other; they look after each other in large and small ways. Adults shelter and protect children. Children try to be kind and loving to the grownups, knowing how important this is to the grownups.

These families, and all other families, have problems, fights. People are disappointed in each other. People fail each other. Kids get angry and say and do hurtful things. So do parents. Kids want their parents to be perfect, but they aren't. Parents make mistakes. They don't always do what's best for their children, because they have needs and problems of their own.

Some families have overwhelming difficulties. Money problems, health problems, job problems, problems between the grownups, all make life hard for the kids. Kids who are unhappy make life hard for the adults. But mostly the kids survive; they are strong and tough, and they learn a great deal from the bad experiences as well as from the good ones.

After all, we're all experts on the subject; we all came from families, and we all care about them. We all can try to exercise wisdom and choice in forming and sustaining families we love.

Postscript

This book began as a photographic exhibition at The Children's Museum in Boston, Massachusetts. Many families joined the project, allowing me to photograph and interview them, generously sharing their feelings and ideas. Kids spoke of their problems, pleasures, interests, and hopes, and carefully corrected and approved my edited versions of their taped conversations.

In the finished exhibit, a table with paper, crayons, and pencils encouraged visitors to join the show. Kids made drawings and stories about their own families and put them up on the walls. Many were joyous: "I have a family and they love me; that's the way it's going to be." Others expressed the pain of family problems in pictures and words: "I wish I had a nice family. If your parents are divorced, be thankful!"

One visitor asked, "I have only one question. Is it wrong to be idealistic and want a traditional family with a mom and dad, a couple of kids, a dog and a cat, and grandparents who live in St. Louis?"

And another replied, "No. This exhibit makes no judgment in regard to right and wrong. It acknowledges that there are many kinds of families in addition to the traditional one."

One teenager found help: "When I first found out about my daddy being gay I was very upset, but after seeing what you have about being gay I feel a lot better about his sexual preferences. Thank you sooo much."

And many people voiced this sentiment: "The photographs show that the traditional family unit is changing; however, this transition is preserving the only really important ingredient to make a family — love."

Adults wrote about their own experiences and opinions, and posted these:

"I've been part of a big family, a single-parent (me) family, and a traditional family. I think it's all the same! . . . I think that if you love someone you have to work at it. That can relate to 1 other person or 100 other people. And we are all in the *human* family."

"Families are precious! The diversity here makes me realize the strength, the willingness and bondedness that hold us together. To be unique, irreplaceable and unrepeatable, that is family. Color, size, denomination or preferences only add flavor and texture to a beautiful commodity."

Further Readings

Adoff, Arnold. *All the Colors of the Race*. New York: Lothrop, Lee and Shepard, 1982. (Grades 4–8)

Berman, Claire, ill. by Dick Wilson. *"What am I Doing in a Step-Family?"* Secaucus, N.J.: Lyle Stuart, 1982. (Grades 3–7)

Bosche, Susanne, trans. by Louis Mackay, photographs by Andreas Hansen. *Jenny Lives with Eric and Martin*. Boston: Gay Men's Press, 1983. (Kindergarten–grade 2)

Bradley, Buff, ill. by Maryann Cocca. *Where Do I Belong? A Kids' Guide to Stepfamilies*. Reading, Mass.: Addison-Wesley, 1982. (Grades 3–7)

Bunin, Catherine, and Sherry Bunin. *Is That Your Sister? A True Story of Adoption*. New York: Pantheon, 1976. (Grades 1–4)

Caines, Jeannette, ill. by Steven Kellogg. *Abby*. New York: Harper, 1973. (Preschool–grade 2)

———, ill. by Ronald Himler. *Daddy*. New York: Harper, 1977. (Preschool–grade 3)

Dolmetsch, P., and A. Shih, eds. *The Kids' Book About Single-Parent Families*. New York: Doubleday, 1985. (Grades 5–9)

Dragonwagon, Crescent, ill. by Arieh Zeldich. *Always, Always*. New York: Macmillan, 1984. (Grades 1–4)

Drescher, Joan. *Your Family, My Family*. New York: Walker, 1980. (Grades 2–5)

Getzoff, Ann, and Carolyn McClenahan. *Step Kids: A Survival Guide for Teenagers in Stepfamilies*. New York: Walker, 1984. (Grades 6–10).

Girard, Linda W., ill. by Judith Friedman. *Adoption Is for Always*. Niles, Ill.: Whitman, 1986. (Kindergarten–grade 3)

Greenberg, Judith E., and Helen H. Carey, photographs by Barbara Kirik. *Adopted*. New York: Watts, 1987. (Kindergarten–grade 4)

Greenfield, Eloise. *Grandmama's Joy*. New York: Philomel/Putnam, 1980. (Grades 3–4)

Holz, Loretta. *Foster Child*. New York: Messner, 1984. (Grades 2–5)

Ives, Sally Blakeslee, David Fassler, and Michele Lwash. *The Divorce Workbook: A Guide for Kids and Families*. Burlington, Vt.: Waterfront, 1985. (Preschool–grade 3)

Krementz, Jill. *How It Feels When Parents Divorce*. New York: Knopf, 1984. (Grades 3–8)

Lexau, Joan M., pictures by Robert Weaver. *Me Day*. New York: Dial, 1971. (Preschool–grade 3)

Nickman, Steven L., ill. by Diane de Groat. *When Mom and Dad Divorce*. New York: Messner, 1986. (Grades 3–7)

Perry, Patricia, and Marietta Lynch. *Mommy and Daddy Are Divorced*. New York: Dial, 1978. (Preschool–grade 3)

Rofes, Eric, ed. *The Kids' Book of Divorce: By, For and About Kids*. New York: Vintage, 1982. (Grades 4–8)

Rosenberg, Maxine B., photographs by George Ancona. *Being Adopted*. New York: Lothrop, Lee and Shepard, 1984. (Grades 1–4)

Severance, Jane, ill. by Jan Jones. *Lots of Mommies*. Chapel Hill, N.C.: Lollipop Power, 1984. (Kindergarten–grade 4)

———, ill. by Tea Schook. *When Megan Went Away*. Chapel Hill, N.C: Lollipop Power, 1979. (Kindergarten–grade 2)

Simon, Norma, ill. by Joe Lasker. *All Kinds of Families*. Niles, Ill.: Whitman, 1976. (Preschool–grade 3)

———, ill. by Arieh Zeldich. *I Wish I Had My Father*. Niles, Ill.: Whitman, 1983. (Kindergarten–grade 3)

Sobol, Harriet Langsam, photographs by Patricia Agre. *My Other-Mother, My Other-Father*. New York: Macmillan, 1979. (Grades 3–7)

———, photographs by Patricia Agre. *We Don't Look Like Our Mom and Dad*. New York: Coward, 1984. (Kindergarten–grade 4)

Tax, Meredith, ill. by Marylin Hafner. *Families*. Boston: Little, Brown, 1981. (Preschool–grade 3)